The Fulfillment of Prophecy

By Chester K. Lehman

Professor of Theology
Eastern Mennonite Seminary, Harrisonburg, Virginia

 HERALD PRESS, SCOTTDALE, PENNSYLVANIA

THE FULFILLMENT OF PROPHECY
Copyright © 1971 by Herald Press, Scottdale, Pa. 15683
Published 1950. Revised 1971
International Standard Book Number: 0-8361-1649-6
Printed in the United States

To My Beloved Wife

Who labors with me as a true Helpmeet

Who shares the convictions which gave birth to this testimony

Who partakes of the burden bound up in this message

This book is affectionately dedicated

Contents

1. Introduction 7
2. Some Fundamental Principles
    of Interpretation 8
3. Some Rules of Interpretation 14
4. The Fundamental Starting Point
    in the Study of the
    Fulfillment of Prophecy 18
5. The Kingdom 21
6. The Church 30
7. God's Program of the Future 31
8. Israel's Future 37
9. Do the Scriptures Predict a Literal
    Restoration of Mosaism? 40
10. Do the Scriptures Predict a Literal
    Restoration of Edenic Conditions? . . . 42
11. The Interpretation of Revelation 43
12. The Church's Interpretation of the
    Fulfillment of Prophecy 49
13. The Fundamental Issues Involved 52
    Bibliography 60

1. Introduction

The fulfillment of predictive prophecy stands as one of the central pillars of evidence that the Scriptures are the very word of God. God alone is omniscient; therefore words of omniscience are God-breathed.

We enter still deeper into the wonders of the foretelling of future events by noting its purpose. When our first parents were receiving judgment for their sin, God held before them a hope of deliverance from the bondage of their sin. God promised that the seed of the woman would crush the head of the serpent. This predictive promise inspired faith in a God-provided salvation. It gave stamp to the nature of predictive prophecy; prophecy had to do with building up hope in God's redemption.

Very early in the study of this subject, problems of interpretation are encountered which require Holy Spirit illumination for their solution. The fulfillments of predictions do not always correspond with what we might think the fulfillments would be. We are plunged at once into a careful study of the principles of interpretation in order that the proper path through these studies might be mapped out. It is also soon observed that differing views of prophecy are not mere differences of interpretation of so many Scriptures; they represent well-defined systems of interpretation and theological viewpoints. This situation also makes imperative the establishing of certain fundamental principles of interpretation and the recognition of accurate rules of interpretation.

Obviously there is great need for humility and reserve in the interpretation of prophecy. Bias, prejudice, and carnality defy the illumination of the Holy Spirit. It should not be necessary to add that the Scriptures themselves are the best guide to the interpretation of prophecy.

2. Some Fundamental Principles of Interpretation

Only by the application of true principles of interpretation can an accurate interpretation of the Scriptures be made. The most basic principles concern the place of the Old Testament and its relation to the New Testament. This may be expressed in five statements.

1. The Old Testament is inspired and hence authoritative. Matthew 4:4-10; 5:18; John 10:35; 2 Timothy 3:15, 16; 2 Peter 1:21.

This principle is drawn from the Old Testament's own claims concerning its origin as well as from the testimony of Christ and the apostles. Fully seven eighths of the content of the Pentateuch (excluding Genesis) is definitely ascribed to God through His mouthpiece, Moses. Prophets claim that their words come from God. In like manner Christ regards the Old Testament as the rule of faith and life. Through the multitude of quotations from the Old Testament, the apostles declare their attitude with regard to its authority. This authority should be held securely in thought as additional principles of relationship between the Testaments are given.

2. *The Old and New Testaments possess grand unity and harmony of thought and teaching.* Matthew 5:17-19; 13:14; John 5:39; Romans 4:3-8; Ephesians 1:9, 10; Hebrews 1:1, 2.

Since all Scripture is God-breathed, perfect unity and harmony is found in all its parts. Christ did not come to destroy the Law or the prophets but to fulfill them. In a very fundamental way New Testament doctrines are based on Old Testament teaching, thus proving their harmony. The following principles do not nullify biblical unity.

3. *The Old Testament is the preparation for the New.*

First, there is depicted in prophecy a conscious preparation in the Old Testament for the New.

Beginning with the first promise of redemption in Genesis 3:15 and continuing to the last prediction in Malachi 4:5 one grand procession of prophecies converge in Christ and the covenant He instituted.

Second, the New Testament furnishes abundant evidence that the Old prepared for the New. All the references to the Old Testament are so many proofs of this preparation. Among the multitude of such connections, the institution of the New Covenant, the outpouring of the Holy Spirit, the high-priestly work of Christ, His enthronement, and the universal mission of the gospel — all were foretold in the Old and thus prepared the way for the New. There is also an expressive list of words such as *example, pattern, figure, shadow,* and *type,* whose use in the New Testament indicates that the Old typifies the New. Thus the authoritative Old Testament which with the New Testament constitutes a grand unity and harmony is to be viewed nevertheless as a preparation for the New.

4. The Old Testament was fulfilled and displaced by the New Testament. Matthew 5:17-45; 9:16, 17; 19:8, 9; Luke 16:16; John 1:17; Romans 10:4; Galatians 3:19, 25; 4:4, 5, 31; Hebrews 7:11, 12, 18, 19, 22; 8:6-8, 13.

While on the one hand Christ said that He did not come to destroy the Law or the prophets but to fulfill them; on the other hand He placed His teaching over against that of the Old Testament. He would not put new wine into old bottles or a patch of new cloth on an old garment. The Law and the prophets were until John; with Christ the era of the kingdom of God began. In Hebrews the change from the Aaronic priesthood to that of Christ was made because the former was inefficient. The Law was disannulled because of its weakness and unprofitableness. The Old Covenant by reason of its age and decay was superseded by the New.

5. *The New Covenant is final.*

The New Covenant is not one new disclosure to be followed by others; it is rather the consummate disclosure beyond which there remains no covenant to be made. The very word, "new," denotes superiority in kind and finality. Every covenant is made with the shedding of blood and there is no blood higher than Christ's to shed. After the Son has spoken, there is no higher one to speak. In further proof of the finality of the New Covenant let us note:

a. There are no statements in the New Testament of successive or greater fulfillments beyond those which pertain to the New Covenant. (1) There is no statement that Elijah will yet come in person; Christ said he has come in the person of John. He gives no hint of a future appearance. (2) In the institution of the New Covenant no covenant remains to be established.

(3) There is no promise either in the Old or New Testament of a second outpouring of the Holy Spirit; the Holy Spirit has come. (4) There is no reference to any kingdom other than Christ's present spiritual and the Father's future eternal kingdoms. (5) There is no reference to Christ's receiving kingly authority in the future; He is already enthroned and now possesses all authority in heaven and on earth. (6) There is no prediction of a still more universal diffusion of the gospel than that under the New Covenant. (7) There is no promise of an era of salvation beyond that of the New Covenant; the ultimate that the prophets saw was the residue of men seeking the Lord and all the Gentiles upon whom God's name is called. When the gospel is preached in all the world, the end shall come. (8) There are no unfulfilled prophecies concerning Christ or Israel which are not comprehended under the New Covenant.

b. All New Testament predictions point to the present as the last age of the world. Matthew 13:40; 24:14; Acts 2:17; 1 Corinthians 10:11; Hebrews 1:2, 5, 9; 9:26; 1 Peter 1:20, 21; 1 John 2:18. According to Christ this age ends in the consummation. We are now in "the last days." "Upon us are come the ends of the world." The end shall come when the gospel is preached in all the world. Christ's first appearing was in the *end of the world* and in *these last times;* no age succeeds the *end of the world,* and *the last times.*

c. All New Testament predictions point to imminent consummation and not to the introduction of another age in this world. Matthew 13: 39-43, 49, 50; 24:6, 13, 14; 1 Corinthians 15:24, 52; 1 Thessalonians 5:2, 3; Hebrews 12:26, 27; 1 Peter 4:7; 2 Peter 3:10-13; Revelation 22:20. The present era is that of the preaching of the gospel to all nations. Its accomplishment brings *the end*, the consummation. The time of the resurrection is at *the last trump;* there is no *trump* to succeed the last one. In the unfolding of prophetic times the last trump ushers in the consummation and not another age. According to Hebrews the next prophetic unfolding is the shaking of the earth and heaven, the time when the things that are made shall pass away so that the things which cannot be shaken may remain. Peter writes pointedly, "The end of all things is at hand." He states that the course of this world will be suddenly broken into by the day of the Lord in which the material universe shall be destroyed and the new heavens and new earth shall be created.

d. The New Covenant is eternal. Isaiah 55:3; 61:8; Jeremiah 32:40; 50:5; Ezekiel 16:60; 37:26; Hebrews 13:20. It is eternal: (1) because it is *new*; (2) because it has accomplished the actual forgiveness of sins as foretold by Jeremiah (31: 34; cf. Heb. 10:17, 18); and (3) because there remains no predicted covenant to supersede it.

3. Some Rules of Interpretation

1. Christian doctrine is based on unfigurative language, although figurative language may contribute to the truth.

The parable of the ten virgins does not lead to the conclusion that half of mankind shall be saved and half lost. The point of the parable is that of the necessity of being ready for His coming.

The parable of the sower becomes very meaningful in the light of Jesus' interpretation of it. Only on the basis of His explanation may we conclude that the details given by Jesus are actually set forth in the parable. Matthew 13:3-8, 18-23. The same is true in the parable of the weeds. Matthew 13:24-30, 36-43. Certainly some of the details of the parable are evident to the reader, but Jesus' explanation gives actuality to the fundamental truths therein set forth.

2. Language means what it says in the intent of the original writer.

Since, however, such great import is attached to the meaning of Scripture, special pains must be taken to ascertain what it says. Surely Christ did not mean that if one's eye offends him he should literally pluck it out. People with gouged out eyes could be just as lustful as with them. Obviously Christ meant "cut off the evil desire."

3. Allegorizing or spiritualizing Scripture is an entirely erroneous method of interpretation.

This method regards unfigurative language as figurative. Its only limitation is the imagination of the interpreter.

4. Exceeding great care must be exercised in discriminating between figurative language and that which is not. When a given portion is found to be figurative, the specific rules which belong to each kind of figure must then be applied.

We need to grant biblical writers and speakers the same liberty of using figures as we allow ourselves, and to apply the same commonsense principles of interpretation as we do in common speech. We need to remember also that the Hebrew language and mode of speech in contrast with ours was pictorial rather than abstract.

With particular reference to the vision we need to remember that the details of the vision do not constitute the details of the truth taught. Thus in the dream-visions of the butler, baker, Pharaoh, Daniel, Nebuchadnezzar, and Ezekiel, which are interpreted, the details of the vision are not the details of the truth taught.

Turning to the Book of Revelation we encounter first the problem of discriminating between figurative and nonfigurative language. A definite clue to the language of *vision* occurs in the opening verses. God *showed* certain things to John, and he *saw* them. Everything *shown* and *seen* is a vision. Samples of visions thus introduced are 1:11; 4:1, 2; 5:1; 6:1; 7:1; 20:1; 21:1. From this it will be seen that the greater portion of the book is in the language of vision. In direct contrast with this, however, there are two entire chapters (2, 3) which are simple letters, hence nonfigurative.

The bearing of this on the interpretation of Revelation becomes very apparent in two directions. That interpretation which regards the visions as literal breaks down at once as not giving us the sense of Scripture. Further, that interpretation which regards the letters to the seven churches as figurative also fails to give the sense of Scripture. How crucial this matter becomes in the interpretation of the book will now appear. One interpretation regards the seven churches of Asia as prophetic of seven periods of church history. This is plainly to allegorize Scripture. When chapters four to the end are regarded in a general way as literal, the sense of Scripture is again missed. Among others we are compelled to deal with some very knotty problems associated, say, with the thousand-year reign. The binding of the devil, a spiritual being, with a literal chain, the first resurrection, the second death, the loosing of the devil for a season, and the battle of Gog and Magog, almost defy interpretation on a literal basis. While the interpretation of this portion as a vision presents difficulties almost as great, the fact remains that it bears the marks of being a vision and, therefore, regardless of the difficulty encountered, it must be interpreted as a vision if the sense of Scripture is to be gained.

The outcome of allegorizing chapters 2 and 3 and of literalizing chapters 4 to 22, in its bearing on doctrine, is clear. The program of the future becomes something like this: the seven churches of Asia become seven periods of church history and thus the Laodicean church is placed just prior to our Lord's return. John's being caught up to heaven is made to symbolize the "rapture" of the church. Chapters 4 to 19 are taken to describe a period of seven years following the "rapture." Chapter 19 is understood to picture another phase of Christ's return, the revelation; and chapter 20 a reign of 1,000 years after this event.

On the other hand when chapters 2 and 3 are taken as letters to seven churches, and chapters 4 to 22 as largely composed of visions, an entirely different program of the future is obtained. John's being caught up to glory is understood to mean that he was caught up in the spirit and allowed to see things which were to come to pass in the world after his time, that is, during the era of the church. While the world appears chaotic to the church on earth, John is allowed to see that all things are under the control of our reigning Lord. He is leading world affairs

17

forward to consummation in final judgment at His return. Thus chapters 4 to 20 describe the course of world history from Pentecost until our Lord's return for judgment. This portion of the book is designed for the church in tribulation and serves to brace Christians for the life and death struggle with the forces of evil. Chapters 21 and 22 take their beginning after final judgment when the former things are passed away.

4. The Fundamental Starting Point in the Study of the Fulfillment of Prophecy

1. The starting point for building up a scriptural interpretation of the fulfillment of prophecy is found in the Old Testament expressions THE LATTER DAYS, the LAST DAYS, AFTERWARD, and IN THAT DAY. Genesis 49:1; Numbers 24:14-17; Deuteronomy 4:30; 31:29; Isaiah 2:2; Micah 4:1; Jeremiah 23:20; 30:24; 48:47; 49:39; Ezekiel 38:16; Hosea 3:5; Daniel 10:14; Joel 2:28; Amos 9:11.

According to the Old Testament, time was divided into two eras: the present age and the last days or the Messianic age. The prophets saw imminent judgment upon their nation as well as upon others, but in the future the Anointed One should come. His coming marked off a new era. The prophets were granted the privilege of seeing some of the glories of the time of the Messiah. Together their glimpses form one grand composite picture of the *last days* in which Messiah should reign. The prophets saw no third age beyond the "last days." This may be shown by a diagram as follows:

The Present Age	The Last Days, the Days of
(That in which the prophets lived)	the Messiah

2. *The New Testament prophetic revelation builds directly on this Old Testament distinction.* Acts 2:17; 15:15, 16; Hebrews 1:2; 2:5; 9:26; 1 Peter 1:20, 21; 1 John 2:18.

More emphatic than merely to say something is fulfilled, Peter uses language of identification: "This is that which was spoken by the prophet Joel." He refers to the time of Christ's first coming as *these last times*, and John refers to his day as *the last time*. In Hebrews the writer preserves the Old Testament distinction, according to which the time of God's speaking through His Son is in the *last of these days* (A.R.V.). The *world to come* of Old Testament prophecy is subjected to Christ; and as he explains, "We see Jesus . . . crowned with glory and honour." The conclusion to which these Scriptures lead is that the present time (from Pentecost to the end) is the last days of Old Testament prophecy. What the prophets spoke concerning the age of the Messiah is now being gloriously fulfilled.

3. *The New Testament divides the last days into two parts: THE PRESENT WORLD and THE WORLD TO COME.* Matthew 12:32; 13:39, 40, 49; Mark 10:30; Luke 18:30; 20:34-36; Romans 8:38; 1 Corinthians 3:22; Galatians 1:4; Ephesians 1:21; 2:2, 7; 1 Timothy 4:8; 6:17-19.

The present world is temporal and limited to things of this life. The world to come is eternal, being inaugurated by the resurrection. In the *world to come* they neither marry nor are given in marriage. Timothy is enjoined to charge them that are rich in *this world* (age) to lay up in store a good foundation against *the time to come.* The New Testament knows of no age intervening *the present world* and *the world to come.* This may be shown by diagram as follows:

The Last Days

Christ's Second Coming *and* the Resurrection

This World	The World to Come
(begins with Christ's first coming)	*(begins at Christ's return)*

Into this prophetic framework of time eras falls the New Testament teaching concerning the kingdom. The present kingdom belongs to *this world* and is temporal, while the future kingdom belongs to the *world to come* and is eternal.

5. The Kingdom

1. The Fundamental Questions.

At the opening of Christ's ministry He declared "the kingdom of God is at hand." Matthew 3:2; Mark 1:15. At least four questions press for solution:

a. What kingdom does Christ announce? Is it spoken of by the prophets?

b. Did Christ establish the kingdom He announced?

c. What is the relation of the kingdom which He established to the Messianic kingdom spoken of by the prophets?

d. Did the Old Testament foresee the church?

2. The kingdom announced by the Evangelists, the Baptist, and Christ is the Messianic kingdom of prophecy. Mark 1:1-3, 15; Luke 4:17-19.

Mark chooses two Messianic kingdom prophetic contexts in order to identify the Baptist and his work. The first is Malachi 3:1, where he acclaimed the messenger who is preparing the way for the Messiah. The second is Isaiah 40:3, in which the Baptist is held to be the forerunner of the Messiah. Christ declares that the time is fulfilled; that is, the time for the fulfillment of the prophecies had come. In the synagogue at Nazareth, Christ lays claim to fulfilling Isaiah's grand prediction of being the one anointed to preach good tidings. He more than anyone else in the New Testament spoke of the day of vengeance (Matthew 5:22; 13:41, 49, 50; 24:37-51; 25:41-46). Further, Christ built the second beatitude directly on Isaiah's words, "to comfort all that mourn." These are also Messianic kingdom contexts.

3. *Christ established the kingdom which He announced.*

Christ and the apostles went everywhere preaching the gospel of the kingdom. Uniformly He taught that there is a present aspect of the kingdom. The kingdom is the present possession of the poor in spirit and of those persecuted for righteousness' sake. We are bidden to seek first the kingdom of God. In each of the parables of Matthew 13 the kingdom is spoken of as a present reality. The present kingdom is called Christ's kingdom, while the future kingdom is that of the Father (Matthew 13:41-43; John 18:36; Acts 2:33-36; 1 Corinthians 15:25-28; Colossians 1:13).

4. *Evidences which identify the present kingdom with the Messianic kingdom of prophecy.*

The law of identity is appealed to here. In the prophetic Scriptures a multitude of predictions portray the kingdom of the Messiah. By means of these several prophetic pictures the New Testament seeks to establish the identity of the kingdom established by Christ with that of prophecy. Each Old Testament picture presented is recognized by students of all schools of interpretation as referring to the Messianic kingdom. When the New Testament uses language of identification such as *this is that, to this agrees,* or *thus is fulfilled,* which was spoken by the prophet, it follows that the kingdom established is the Messianic kingdom.

a. The Messenger; Malachi 3:1; Mark 1:2. Malachi 3:1-6 is a Messianic kingdom context. Since John is acclaimed the messenger of the Messiah, he prepared the way for the Messianic kingdom.

b. The Forerunner. Isaiah 40:3-5; Mark 1:1-3. Isaiah prophesies concerning the forerunner of the Messianic king. The King follows the forerunner.

c. Elijah sent to prepare the way for the Messiah and to restore all things. Malachi 4:5; Matthew 11:14; 17:11, 12. The coming of Elijah is closely connected with the establishment of the Messianic kingdom. Christ asserts that John is Elijah. In the unfolding of the prophecies Elijah does come first and restores all things; but Christ says, "Elias is come already." The Messianic kingdom followed in the wake of the Baptist's work.

d. The sign of the Messiah. Zechariah 9:9; Matthew 21:4, 5. Zechariah gave a sign whereby Israel might know their King. Christ's act of fulfilling this sign was His claim to being their King.

e. The making of the New Covenant. Isaiah 55:3; Jeremiah 31:31; Ezekiel 37:26; Matthew 26:28; 1 Corinthians 11:25; 2 Corinthians 3:6, 14; Hebrews 8:6 — 10:18; 13:20. The making of the Old Covenant instituted the Old Testament theocracy. In the same manner the making of the New Covenant establishes the New Testament Christocracy. The tenor of the entire Epistle to the Hebrews, and especially of its central section, 8:6 — 10:18, speaks with clarion voice that our Lord instituted the covenant foretold by Jeremiah. He closes the epistle with the sublime benediction, 13:20, 21, in which the eternal covenant established by Christ is identified with that spoken of by Isaiah and Ezekiel. Since Christ instituted the New Covenant, His reign has begun. If the New Covenant is not yet made, we are still under the Old and subject to the Mosaic Law.

f. The universal mission of the gospel. Isaiah 49:6; Joel 2:32; Amos 9:12; Matthew 24:14; 28:19, 20; Acts 2:21; 13:47; 15:17. One of the glories of the messianic kingdom is the extension of the gospel to the Gentiles. A striking phenomenon is observed here. On the one side, not in all the Old Testament or in the New Testament until the eve of Christ's ascension was anyone sent to Gentiles with a gospel message. On the other side, in the Old Testament a continuous stream of prophecies of the worldwide mission of the gospel during the reign of the Messiah is given. In giving the Great Commission Christ, who had received the "all power" of the Messiah, is asserting that the time of the universal mission of the gospel had come. When the gospel shall be preached in all the world, the end shall come. Peter identifies the present universal mission of the gospel with the prophecy of Joel, and James with that of Amos. The New Testament knows of no other era of worldwide dissemination of the gospel beyond this one.

g. The acceptable year of the Lord, the day of salvation. Isaiah 49:8; 61:1, 2; Luke 4:19; Acts 3:18, 19; 2 Corinthians 6:2. Not only does the Old Testament look forward to the universal mission of the gospel in the Messianic kingdom; it also regards the time of this kingdom as being specifically "the acceptable year of the Lord" and the great day of salvation. Christ is the first to make this identification and is followed by Paul in the words, "Now is the accepted time, now is the day of salvation." There is no New Testament prediction of a "day of salvation" beyond this one. Christ's return is for final judgment and not for the establishing of the "day of salvation."

h. The outpouring of the Holy Spirit. Isaiah 32:15; 44:3; Ezekiel 37:14; 39:29; Joel 2:28; Acts 2:16. Another identifying mark of the Messianic kingdom is the outpouring of the Holy Spirit. Peter says, "This is that which was spoken by the prophet Joel," and then quotes Joel 2:28-32. The prediction holds in view the coming of the Spirit and the time when "whosoever shall call on the name of the Lord shall be saved." The language, "this is that," is the strongest possible way of asserting identity between prediction and fulfillment.

i. The Messiah enthroned. Numbers 24:7; 2 Samuel 7:12-16; Psalm 110:1; Isaiah 9:6, 7; 11:10; Daniel 7:13, 14; Zechariah 6:13; Matthew 28:18; Luke 22:69; John 18:36; Acts 2:33-36; 5:31; 7:56; Romans 8:34; 15:9-12; 1 Corinthians 15:24-28; Ephesians 1:20-23; 2:6; Philippians 2:9-11; Colossians 1:13; 3:1; 1 Timothy 6:15; Hebrews 1:3; 2:9; 8:1; 10:12, 13; 12:2; 1 Peter 3:22; Revelation 1:5; 3:21; 5:5, 12, 13; 7:17; 17:14; 19:16; 20:1-10. The climax of Old Testament predictions of the Messianic kingdom is those speaking of His actual enthronement. The throne of David is the type of Christ's throne. God gave David the right to rule in His stead. David's was a transferred authority. Psalm 110 defines the Messianic kingship. According to this prophecy and Paul's testimony in 1 Corinthians 15:25, when Christ sits at the right hand of the Father, He is ruling as Messiah and is sitting on David's throne. The New Testament takes great pains to state that the kingship now exercised by Christ is that foretold by the prophets. Christ says, "All power (authority) is given unto me." Peter says that the sending of the Holy Spirit is evidence of Christ's exaltation, it being the first act of His kingship. In most emphatic language Peter concludes, "Therefore let all the house of Israel know assuredly, that God hath made that same Jesus . . . both Lord and Christ." What more explicit statement could be made than that the Anointed One, the Messiah, the Christ, has been anointed and reigns! Peter says that Christ "is gone into heaven, and is on the right hand of God; angels and authorities and powers being made subject unto him." In order to clinch for Gentile readers their equal privileges with the Jews in the gospel, Paul quotes the familiar Messianic kingship passage from Isaiah, "There shall be a root of Jesse, and he that shall rise to reign over the Gentiles; in him shall the Gentiles trust." The present participation of the Gentiles in the blessings of the gospel is proof that Christ has been enthroned as the Messiah. Elsewhere he says that God "set him at his own right hand . . . far above all principality, and power, and might, and dominion." The Father "hath translated us into the kingdom of his dear Son." This can be none other than the Messianic kingdom.

The simultaneousness of Christ's priestly and kingly works pictured by Psalm 110 and Zechariah 6:13 is fittingly described in Hebrews 1:3; 6:20 where He is pictured as having "sat down on the right hand of the Majesty on high," and of having entered within the veil, "made an high priest for ever after the order of Melchisedec." See the brief but fundamental prophecy of Zechariah 6:13, "priest upon his throne"; and then note Paul's statement, "who is even at the right hand of God, who also maketh intercession for us" (Romans 8:34).

j. The tabernacle of David built again. Amos 9:11; Acts 15:16, 17. The Prophet Amos predicted the rebuilding of the tabernacle of David in order "that the residue of men might seek after the Lord, and all the Gentiles, upon whom my name is called." By James' quoting this prophecy he places the capsheaf to the argument that the Gentile conversions through the preaching of the apostles were proof, that David's tabernacle had been rebuilt; or else how could the gospel come to the Gentiles? Thus the rebuilding of David's tabernacle is spoken of by Amos as the establishment of the Messianic kingdom.

k. The chosen generation, the royal priesthood, the holy nation, the peculiar people. Exodus 19:5, 6; Isaiah 61:6; 1 Peter 2:9. The privileges of Israel under the theocracy typify the privileges of the church under the Christocracy.

l. My People. Hosea 1:10; Romans 9:25, 26; 1 Peter 2:10. Hosea's picture of the Messianic kingdom is fulfilled when God's people shall no longer be called Loruhamah (unpitied) and Loammi (not my people), but they shall be called

Ruhamah (pitied) and Ammi (my people). Both Paul and Peter speak of the fulfillment of this in present time, applying it to both Jews and Gentiles.

Thus the church is now the Israel of God (Galatians 6:16). Peter writes that the promise of the Holy Spirit is to Israel and *"to all that are afar off, even as many as the Lord our God shall call."* Paul draws distinction between Israelites by blood and Israelites by faith, "For they are not all Israel, which are of Israel" (Romans 9:1-6). In Christ the church constitutes the commonwealth of Israel, being composed of Jew and Gentile alike, fellow citizens with the saints and of the household of God (Ephesians 2:11-22).   ° ° °

To what conclusion do these twelve strands of prophetic teaching lead? They are not cases where one or two Scriptures might be bent to mean that the Messianic kingdom has been established, but rather of a great multitude of biblical statements whose explicit purpose is to identify the present reality with the prophecy of it. The Old Testament gives so many prophetic pictures of the Messianic kingdom; the New Testament seeks to show their fulfillment in present time. On the basis of these evidences it appears to be the plain sense of Scripture that Christ established the Messianic kingdom. There is not a single Scripture which says that it is not yet established.

6. The Church

Here I desire to note that the Old Testament foresaw the church and prepared the way for it. All the foregoing evidences of the establishment of the Messianic kingdom are so many proofs that the Old Testament predicted the church. While it is true according to Ephesians 3:4-11 that the full idea of the church could not be understood until its revelation in Paul's ministry, these evidences prove that the present era is not a valley between two mountain peaks of prophecy, the first and second comings, respectively, of Christ, and unseen by the prophets. The church is not a detached organism without any connection in prophecy, an afterthought in God's plan. Rather it is central in the unfolding purposes of God. It is bound up warp and woof in the prophetic Scriptures. It is itself the mountain peak, or better, the plateau of fulfilled prophecy. Observe how Peter confirmed this: "But ye are a chosen generation, a royal priesthood, an holy nation, a peculiar people; that ye should shew forth the praises of him who hath called you out of darkness into his marvellous light: which in time past were not a people, but are now the people of God: which had not obtained mercy, but now have obtained mercy" (1 Peter 2:9, 10).

7. God's Program of the Future

Let us now trace the teaching of the New Testament as regards the unfolding of future events. To build up the program of the future on the basis of Old Testament Scriptures alone exposes us to the danger of ascribing to Christ's second coming what properly belongs to the first. New Testament teachings are given in the light of the meaning of Christ's first coming and hence furnish the safest guide to the program of the future. A process of subtracting the fulfilled from unfulfilled prophecies in the Old Testament and then of referring the remainder to the future without consulting the predictions given in the New is equally dangerous:

1. God's program as revealed by Christ. Matthew 13:37-43, 49, 50; 16:27; 19:28, 29; 24; 25; Luke 19:11-27; 21:5-36; John 12:48.

Let us look again at those expressions which furnish the mold into which Christ's teachings take their form: *this world* and *the world to come.* The present age is temporal and is consummated at the Lord's return; the future which immediately succeeds the present is eternal. This age is brought to a close "in the regeneration when the Son of man shall sit in the throne of his glory." The resurrection marks the transition from *this world* to *that world.* The *world to come* introduces a mode of existence in which human relationships shall have ceased.

In Christ's interpretation of the parable of the tares, end-time events are pictured in a few bold strokes. The field is the world. The good seed are the children of the kingdom; but the tares are the children of the wicked one; the harvest is the end of the world (age). As the tares are gathered and burned, in like manner at the end of the world (age) the angels shall gather the wicked out of Christ's kingdom and cast them into a furnace of fire. Then shall the righteous shine forth as the sun in the kingdom of their Father. Thus in Christ's view the separation of the wicked from the just shall take place at the end of the age, at which time the righteous shall pass from Christ's kingdom into that of the Father. The companion parable, that of the drag net, teaches the same truth.

The Olivet Discourse (Matthew 24:3 — 25:46; Luke 21:5-36) gives the most detailed forecast of future events. According to the narrative in Matthew's Gospel, Christ first portrays the nature of events during the present age. When the gospel shall have been preached in all the world, the end shall come. Christ then speaks of the fall of Jerusalem which, by comparing the parallel account in Luke, is found to mark the close of Daniel's seventieth week. Thus Christ unlocks the meaning of a most difficult prophecy.

The seventy weeks are found to be a continuous prophetic era which terminates with the great redemptive work of Christ, His enthronement, and the destruction of the great symbol of the Jewish state, the city of Jerusalem. From the fall of Jerusalem to the end of the age shall be wars and tribulation. Jerusalem shall be "desolate, even until the consummation."

After describing the course of this age to the time of His return (Matthew 24:30, 31), Christ gives appropriate warning concerning the meaning of that event. It shall be like it was in the days of Noah. The opportunity of being saved from the Flood terminated when Noah entered the ark and "the Lord shut him in." In like manner the opportunity of being saved eternally shall terminate when Christ shall gather together His elect at His return. Nine times He says, "Watch and be ready." The reason for this is intensified as Christ pictures the judgment which takes place at His coming. Drawing from the familiar scene of a shepherd dividing the sheep from the goats, Christ states that at His coming all nations shall be gathered before Him and He shall separate them one from another, the wicked going away into everlasting punishment and the righteous into life eternal.

Thus Christ's forecasts of the future give the uniform picture of His present reign, followed by His return for raising the dead and for final judgment.

2. God's program as revealed by Peter. Acts 3:19-21; 2 Peter 1:11; 3:10-13.

At Pentecost, Peter labeled this age as the *last days,* the era when "whosoever shall call on the name of the Lord shall be saved." On this account he calls on Israel to repent so that the "times of refreshing shall come from the presence of the Lord." The "times of refreshing" are also "the times of the restitution of all things." It would seem that these two expressions refer to the same time as "the regeneration" spoken of by Christ, so that all three are associated with Christ's return.

In his second epistle, Peter exhorts his readers to make their calling and election sure so that they will enter into the everlasting kingdom of their Lord and Savior Jesus Christ. He shows that the delay in Christ's return is due to the long-suffering of God. He is not willing that any should perish. Nevertheless "the day of the Lord will come as a thief in the night" in which the material universe shall pass away. On this account we ought to be "in all holy conversation and godliness." We "look for new heavens and a new earth, wherein dwelleth righteousness." It is then that the righteous will shine as the sun in the kingdom of their Father.

Thus Peter's forecasts hold this age to be the time for repentance and salvation; the day of the Lord closes this opportunity and issues in final judgment. The eternal state takes its beginning with the new creation.

3. *God's program as taught by Paul.* 1 Thessalonians 4:13 — 5:11; 2 Thessalonians 1:5-10; 1 Corinthians 15.

The Thessalonian Christians were troubled concerning the dead. Paul assures them that Christ shall bring the saints with Him at the *Parousia* (1 Thessalonians 3:13; 4:14); for the bodies of these shall rise before the living saints shall be glorified. Introducing the larger theme, the day of the Lord, Paul states that it shall come as a thief in the night. The wicked shall not escape the judgment of God. The return which brings comfort to the righteous brings also judgment to the ungodly. It is a taking vengeance on them that know not God.

In 1 Corinthians 15, Paul shows that Christ's reign must continue until all enemies are put under His feet. Since the last enemy death is destroyed at the resurrection, this event marks the close of Christ's reign. He shall then deliver up the kingdom to the Father.

Thus according to Paul's teaching, Christ is now reigning, and this reign will terminate at His second coming. Paul also links together the return, the resurrection, and the final judgment.

4. *God's program as taught by Jude and Hebrews.* Jude 14-18; Hebrews 12:26-29.

Jude warns, "Behold, the Lord cometh . . . to execute judgment upon all." In Hebrews the next great event is the shaking of heaven and earth, and the removing of those things that are shaken. The righteous shall receive a kingdom which cannot be moved. This can be nothing less than the eternal kingdom which Christ invites the righteous to inherit (Matthew 25:34).

5. *God's program as taught in Revelation.* 6:12-17; 11:15-19; 14:14-20; 16:12-21; 19:11-21; 20:7-16.

Christ is viewed as reigning now; He is sitting in the midst of the throne and is unloosing the seals. It seems that six times in the Book of Revelation the period of the church is surveyed and each section closes with a description of the return of Christ. Uniformly this return ushers in final judgment. The advance beyond the return of Christ is found in chapter 21, when it is said, "the former things are passed away."

° ° °

From this vast array of New Testament teaching we conclude that God's program of the future uniformly holds three interlocking events in view: the return of Christ, the resurrection, and the judgment. In not a single New Testament Scripture is it said that He returns to reign as Messiah. Unfigurative New Testament Scriptures neither state nor make room for a thousand-year reign after His return. If His coming is for the establishment of the Messianic kingdom, it would seem that the New Testament should expressly state it. Uniformly Christ's return is presented for the purpose of raising the dead for final judgment and of leading the righteous into life eternal.

8. Israel's Future

A great number of Old Testament Scriptures speak of Israel's apostasy, repentance, and regathering to their land (Deuteronomy 31:1-3; Isaiah 11:11, 12; Jeremiah 16:14, 15; 23:5-8; 24:6; 30:3; Ezekiel 37:20-25; Zechariah 8:7, 8; 10:10-12). What is the meaning of these predictions? The following statements seem to express the sense of the Scriptures:

1. God's covenant with Israel was conditioned on faith and obedience.

Their apostasy led to forfeiture of the promised blessing. On repentance God would again show them favor. All later messages to Israel by reason of their being based on the conditional covenants of Leviticus 26:3-42 and Deuteronomy 28 — 30 are to be interpreted as also conditional.

2. The return from captivity held in it the possibility of complete fulfillment of God's promises, but only a few Jews returned.

Postexilic prophets still hold out the promises

of God, dependent of course on Israel's repentance.

3. *The New Testament is silent on the matter of Israel's return to their land.*

When reasons are sought for this silence, the explanation which seems to comprehend all the facts is that the promises of restoration to their land are dependent on the Old Covenant which terminated at the cross. The New Covenant is spiritual and does not have to do with material blessings associated with the land of Palestine. A converted Jew has no interest in returning to Palestine to a restored Mosaism. He is enjoying the fullness of the spiritual privileges of the Messianic kingdom. To return to Palestine for this purpose would be to stoop to material blessings.

4. *The New Testament treatment of Israel may be summed up in the following Scriptures:* Luke 19:42-44; Matthew 21:42, 43; Luke 12:32; 13:35; 21:24; Romans 11:12-26; Ephesians 2:14-18.

(a) Israel did not know the time of their visitation. Christ's coming had in store all the blessings bound up in the promises. (b) On this account the kingdom was taken from Israel and given to a nation bringing forth the fruits thereof. (c) It was the Father's good pleasure to give the kingdom to the little flock that followed Christ. (d) Israel's house is left desolate until they repent. The great city Jerusalem shall be trodden down until the times of the Gentiles be fulfilled. It appears that the times of the Jews came to a close at the fall of Jerusalem and that the times of the Gentiles would come to a close at our Lord's return. Christ does not say that there shall be a second *times* for the Jews. This does not mean that Israel's opportunity of grace is closed, but rather that the Gentiles are receiving the blessings forfeited by the Jews through their rejection of Christ.

Paul notes that Israel's fall is the riches of the world, and the diminishing of them the riches of the Gentiles; also that the casting away of them is the reconciling of the world. On account of these facts he contemplates the results that would follow if they should be received. Here the apostle sees a vista of possibility bound up in the questions, "How much more their fulness?" and "what shall the receiving of them be, but life from the dead?" These questions intimate that should there be a general repentance among Jews, there would follow Gentile conversions best described as "life from the dead." Paul shows how easy it would be for God to graft Israel in; likewise he warns Gentile Christians of being cast off if they prove unfaithful. Paul clearly states that Israel shall be grafted in if they abide not in unbelief. The mystery which he discloses is that blindness in part is happened to Israel until the fulness of the Gentiles be come in, by which language he probably means that Gentile conversions are filling the breach made by Israel's unbelief and in this manner the "all Israel" of prophecy shall be saved. The distinction between Jew and Gentile no longer possesses any significance, for Christ "hath made both one, and hath broken down the middle wall of partition between us."

9. Do the Scriptures Predict a Literal Restoration of Mosaism?

On the basis of Amos 9:11, 12; Isaiah 66:20, 23; Jeremiah 33:16-22; Ezekiel 45:21-25; Zechariah 14:16 some hold that there shall be a literal restoration of Mosaism in the Messianic kingdom. In reply:

1. The literal fulfillment of these Scriptures proves too much.

A memorial of Christ's redemptive work is proper and scriptural, as we have in the Lord's Supper; but no reason can be found for the reestablishment of rudiments after those elementary forms of worship are fulfilled in Christ.

2. It seems entirely inconsistent with the unfolding of the spiritual relationship between man and God that the spiritual privileges of this age should in the future be shrunk to a rudimentary mode of worship from an age less glorious than this.

We have passed out from that stage in which the place of worship counts. John 4:23, 24.

3. *The reestablishment of Mosaism definitely runs counter to the rent veil of the temple.*

Would the restored temple have a rent veil or would it be sewed up?

4. *The reestablishment of Mosaism runs counter to the finished work of Christ, which is so graphically described in the Epistle to the Hebrews.*

Note especially 7:11, 12, 18; 8:12, 13; 12:22-24. The logic of restored Mosaism is that the final sacrifice has not yet been made and that Christ's blood does not avail to the putting away of sin. In this connection Paul warns that a return to observation of days and months and times and years is a repudiation of Christ's finished work of redemption, Galatians 5:4.

5. *The New Testament has nothing to say concerning a restoration of Mosaism.*

There is, however, rich teaching of the building of a spiritual temple on this earth and of a great assembly in heaven, the glory of which is comparable with the glory of our Lord's finished work. See Ephesians 2:20-22; Hebrews 12:18-24; 1 Peter 2:5.

10. Do the Scriptures Predict a Literal Restoration of Edenic Conditions?

On the basis of Isaiah 11:6-9; 35:1-10; 65:17-25, it is held that Edenic conditions shall be literally restored. It may be replied: In itself there can be no objection to a literal restoration of Eden. But as the Scriptures unfold divine revelation, it becomes increasingly clear that what was literal in Eden is restored in far grander spiritual reality in the new heavens and a new earth. To interpret wolf, lamb, leopard, cow, parched ground, and springs of water as literal is to associate nonmoral with spiritual realities such as God's holy mountain, the earth being full of the knowledge of the Lord, and the way of holiness.

In like manner a closely related series of Scriptures as Psalm 46:4; Joel 3:18; Ezekiel 47:1-12; Zechariah 14:8; Revelation 22:1, 2, if interpreted literally, brings together nonmoral elements on the one side with evident spiritual realities on the other, which does not make sense. Further it appears that Revelation 22 is plainly figurative language; and if it is figurative, it would seem that the entire series is also cast in such language because of their evident close relationship. If the language is figurative, then the streams which make glad the city of God, the fountain flowing forth from the house of the Lord, trees bringing forth new fruit because their waters issued out of the sanctuary, and the living water going out from Jerusalem, are meant to symbolize the spiritual life that issues from Christ, begun in this life and continuing throughout all eternity.

11. The Interpretation of Revelation

1. The divine purpose of the book.

It pertains to the "things which must shortly come to pass." Being a book of prophecy, the Revelation was addressed to the seven churches of Asia for the purpose of strengthening them for the fiery persecutions through which they were passing. It was written by John, their brother and companion in tribulation. In a word the book is an expansion of Christ's words in John's Gospel, "In the world ye shall have tribulation: but be of good cheer; I have overcome the world" (16:33). It seeks to brace the churches for this conflict by granting them a heavenly view of the affairs in this world.

When John is bidden, "Come up hither, and I will shew thee things which must be hereafter" (4:1), he sees the chaos of this world from the viewpoint of God who sits on the throne and of the Lamb standing in the midst of it. The Lamb is counted worthy to loose the seals, which fact shows that all unfolding history is under His

43

direction and control. If Christians must suffer martyrdom, they are granted the glorious privilege of resting before the throne of God. Those bending low in tribulation can know that their prayers are ascending to the throne of God and are being heard. Their oppressors are being ruled by a rod of iron and shall come to awful judgment in the lake of fire.

Forecasts of the devil's final overthrow are found in his being cast out of heaven so that a loud voice can say, "Now is come salvation, and strength, and the kingdom of our God, and the power of his Christ: for the accuser of our brethren is cast down" (12:10). The saints are able to overcome him by the blood of the Lamb. Satan knows his time is short.

Thus it is shown to John that above the storm clouds the sun is shining; Christ is reigning and is bringing ultimate victory out of apparent defeat.

This evident purpose shows that the Book of Revelation is designed for the church of all ages. While it was given primarily for the seven churches of Asia, its prophetic nature extends its value to the entire church. Thus the church from Pentecost to the return of our Lord can find in it comfort and encouragement; it is enabled to understand that the chaos of this world is not according to the heavenly viewpoint. The vision of heaven shows that all is under the perfect control of the Lamb.

2. *The structure of the book.*

One mark of structure of the book is the arrangement on the principle of seven. Thus there are seven churches, seven seals, seven trumpets, and seven vials, which are clearly marked. Some students find seven sevens, but it may be best not to push this structure beyond what is plainly evident.

Another mark of structure is a telescopic or spiral arrangement, i.e., one section develops out of the last part of the preceding section and seems to traverse the same ground as the preceding. Thus the seven trumpets are sounded in the opening of the seventh seal. It appears that the same era of time is traversed in each spiral because each is completed with a description of the return of Christ for final judgment. On comparing these descriptions (6:12-17; 11:15-19; 14:14-20; 16:12-21; 19:11-21, and 20:7-15), striking similarities, sufficient, it seems, to confirm their identity, will be discerned.

Thus the structure of the book leads to the conclusion that the period of time traversed in the several spirals is that of the church age extending to and including our Lord's return. Accordingly chapter 20 carries time forward to the return of Christ and the judgment, while chapter 21 presents the picture of the eternal ages following this.

3. *The interpretation of the book.*

The clue to what is figurative in this book is that which was *shown* to John and what he *saw*. This mode of revelation is commonly called vision. In the interpretation of the *vision* we have discovered that the details of what was seen are not the details of the revelation conveyed by the vision. Thus in the first chapter where John had a vision of the glorified Lord, the details of the vision are not the details of the glorified Christ. Unless this principle is rigidly adhered to, the meaning of the book is entirely missed.

Chapters 2 and 3 present letters to the seven churches of Asia. These are plain letters and are almost devoid of any figures. Consequently they are to be interpreted as literal language. To interpret them as descriptions of eras in church history is to allegorize them. That the Book of Revelation is prophetic in character does not by this fact make every portion of it predictive.

In chapter 4, John is caught up in spirit to heaven and is *shown* things which "must be hereafter." The things shown take their beginning at the time of John. Only on the allegorical interpretation of chapters 2 and 3 can it be held that the portions following take their beginning at the return of Christ. Chapters 4 to 20 picture the church as suffering tribulation and the ungodly as being subjected to awful judgments in order to lead them to penitence.

Chapter 20 is a vision of the binding of Satan, the reign of the saints with Christ, the first resurrection, the loosing of Satan, the conflict of Gog and Magog, the final judgment, and the second death. The multitude of differing interpretations of this passage is sufficient evidence of its difficulty. On this account the student of prophecy should be very reserved in his efforts to interpret this vision. On one point, however, we should be certain: since this bears the marks of a vision, the interpretation must be in harmony with the teaching of unfigurative language elsewhere in the New Testament.

Possibly all the elements of this passage are referred to elsewhere in the New Testament and are set forth in unfigurative language. The binding of the devil may be understood as a figure of the effects of Christ's work upon the devil described in Matthew 12:25-29; John 12:31; Hebrews 2:14; 2 Peter 2:4; and 1 John 3:8. According to Matthew 28:18; Acts 2:36; Ephesians 1:20-23; 1 Peter 3:22; and many others, the reign of Christ began with His ascension. Quoting Psalm 110:1, Paul says that Christ must reign until He has put all enemies under His feet and adds that the last enemy to be destroyed is death. Death is destroyed in the resurrection at His coming (1 Corinthians 15:54-57), and then Christ delivers the kingdom to the Father. The

47

first resurrection may refer to the spiritual resurrection of the believers as described in John 5:25; Romans 6:4-6; Ephesians 2:1-10; and Colossians 3:1. In Ephesians 2:6, Paul regards those who have been quickened as reigning with Christ (see Weymouth translation). The loosing of Satan may refer to his increased activity against the church during the last times. The conflict of Gog and Magog is probably identical with Armageddon and describes a final spiritual conflict of the church against her foes. The great white throne judgment would appear to be the same as that described in Matthew 25:31-46. The second death is the doom of the lost in hell.

A helpful way of approach to the meaning of the *first resurrection* and the *second death* may be seen in the following. In Revelation 20 *first death* and *second resurrection* are not named as such. All agree that *first death* and *second resurrection* are bodily death and resurrection respectively. In like manner all agree that *second death* is a spiritual death. Since the unnamed terms are bodily death and resurrection respectively, and since it is evident that *second death* is spiritual, why should it not be consistent to interpret the other named term, *first resurrection*, as also spiritual?

Chapter 21 takes us into the eternal future when the former things shall have passed away. The most precious description of heaven is in the terms of God's dwelling with man.

12. The Church's Interpretation of the Fulfillment of Prophecy

1. The belief of the early church.

The belief of the church in the age immediately succeeding that of the apostles is admirably set forth in the Apostles' Creed, which in its earliest form may be traced back to about AD 130. Two articles describe their fundamental belief: first, "Sitteth at the right hand of the Father"; and second, "from whence he will come to judge the quick and the dead." The former article is technical language setting forth Christ's entrance upon Messianic kingship; the latter states the purpose of His return, namely for final judgment. The Apostles' Creed neither mentions nor makes room for a thousand-year reign of Christ after His coming. If His *coming to reign* were the common primitive Christian faith, it would seem that this creed would have stated that purpose. On the contrary this most ancient creed asserts Christ's assumption of Messianic kingship at the ascension and that the purpose of His return is for judgment.

Many early Christians held to chiliasm, the view that Christ comes to set up an earthly kingdom at Jerusalem and to reign a thousand years. Papias, a disciple of the Apostle John, the first church father to hold this view, ascribes to Christ a lengthy saying with reference to the fruitfulness of the vintage and of the grain during the millennium. The quotation is evidently from Baruch, a Jewish apocalyptic writer, who wrote about 50 BC. This serious error of Papias displays the untrustworthiness of his testimony with reference to the belief of the Apostle John in regard to a literal thousand-year reign of Christ. Eusebius, who writes about AD 325, places a low value on the testimony of Papias and notes further that later Christians who held this view leaned heavily on him. Two observations may be made concerning this early chiliasm: (1) It is Jewish and not biblical in its origin. Its mold is Jewish apocalyptic thought. The church fathers who held to chiliasm quote these uninspired Jewish writings in support of their views and fail to see the differences between Old Testament prophecies and these Jewish writings. (2) Chiliasm ascribes to Christ's return what these uninspired Jewish writers referred to Messiah's coming. Thus the materialism of Jewish thought prior to Christ's birth was imported more or less bodily into Christian thought by chiliasm and has been a dominant characteristic of this type of thought ever since. Not perceiving the New Testament interpretation of the Old Testament Scriptures, the chiliasts would have the church associate with Christ's return what the Jews living before Christ thought of Christ's advent. This was the most fatal error of the chiliasts. Their materialism soon ran into fanatic excesses so that chiliasm was finally denounced by the church as unscriptural.

All the creeds from the Apostles' Creed to those developing out of the Reformation subscribe to the Apostles' Creed and many explicitly denounce chiliasm.

2. *The belief of the early Mennonite Church.*

As to the Mennonite Church, Menno Simons speaks very plainly of Christ's present Messianic reign.[1] In unmistakable terms he calls regeneration the first resurrection.[2] In like manner the four Mennonite confessions of faith drawn up from 1600 to 1632 are explicit as to Christ's present Messianic reign and of His return for judgment.[3] From the Confession drawn up at Dortrecht note the following: "Finally, concerning the resurrection of the dead, we confess with the mouth, and believe with the heart, according to the Scripture, that in the last day all men who shall then have died, and fallen asleep, shall be awakened and quickened, and shall rise again, through the incomprehensible power of God; and that they together with those who then will still be alive, and who shall be changed in the twinkling of an eye, at the sound of the last trump, shall be placed before the judgment

---

1 *Complete Works of Menno Simons*, pp. 82, 183, 425, 428-432
2 *Ibid.*, pp. 231, 232, 235
3 See *Martyrs Mirror*, pp. 31, 36, 41, 391-393

seat of Christ, and the good be separated from the wicked; that then every one shall receive in his own body according to that he hath done, whether it be good or evil; and that the good or pious, as the blessed, shall be taken up with Christ, and shall enter into life eternal . . . to reign and triumph with Christ forever and ever." Note the explicit language describing the general resurrection issuing in final judgment. The reign of Christ spoken of here is His eternal reign.

Thus the historic position of the Mennonite Church and of the Christian church in general has been consistently that of the Apostles' Creed. Christ is now enthroned. He will come to judge.

13. The Fundamental Issues Involved

If the interpretation of the prophetic Scriptures concerned only the first ten verses of Revelation 20, the differences among the views of the future could be dismissed as entirely of a trivial nature. On the contrary the differences begin with the fundamental principles of interpretation and extend to the attitude that is taken of the Messianic kingdom, of the place of the church in the program of God, and of the purposes of Christ's return. Ultimately these differences affect evangelism and missions. It is necessary that the issues be drawn so that the student of prophecy knows fully what is involved when he adopts a view in prophecy.

1. *The New Covenant.*

The whole body of Messianic prophecies focuses in the making of the New Covenant. If the covenant predicted by Jeremiah has not yet been made, then the covenant made at Sinai is still in force and we are still under the Law. If the New Covenant has been made, it carries with it the establishment of the Messianic kingdom in precisely the same manner as the institution of the Old Covenant inaugurated the theocracy. If the New Covenant has been made, no covenant remains to be instituted. Reasons for this are found in the following: (1) The New Covenant is represented as the eternal covenant. Through it there is actual forgiveness of sins. (2) There is no higher blood than Christ's to be shed for its ratification, and there is no higher person than Christ to ratify another. (3) If another is to be made, the existing covenant must be considered as not having accomplished the purpose of forgiveness of sins.

2. *The restoration of Mosaism.*

The making of the New Covenant abrogated the Old Covenant. If bloody sacrifices are to be reinstituted, the blood of Christ has not availed to the putting away of sin, and it will be necessary to sew up the rent veil of the old temple.

3. *The reign of Christ.*

Through the institution of the New Covenant, Christ established the Messianic kingdom. If Christ is not reigning, He has not been exalted; for His exaltation constitutes His being made Lord and Christ.

4. *The Church.*

By the language "my church" Christ makes a distinction between His church and the Old Testament church. He established the church without regard to the acceptance or rejection of Himself on the part of the Jews. In the church the whole mass of prophecies concerning the Messianic kingdom have been fulfilled. It is the perfected instrument of salvation toward which the entire Old Testament looked. There is no prophetic Scripture which looks to another saving instrument beyond the church. If the church was not seen by the prophets, it is an afterthought in God's plan and loses its basis in the Old Testament stream of prophecy.

5. *The purpose of Christ's return.*

Uniformly the New Testament states that Christ is coming to receive the church unto Himself and to judge the world. The day of grace closes for all mankind when Christ receives to Himself His own. This is the essence of the manifold exhortations given in the New Testament Scriptures. At no point in all the Scriptures is any hope of salvation held out to the unsaved after the homegoing of the church. If Christ's return does not close the opportunity of salvation, where do the Scriptures place its termination?

6. *Evangelism.*

The evangelistic appeal built upon the return of Christ is that of readiness for His coming. Just as the opportunity of being saved from the Flood closed when the Lord shut Noah in the ark, in like manner the opportunity of eternal salvation shall close when He comes for His elect. If this is not true, the chief incentive to evangelism based on our Lord's return disappears.

7. *Missions.*

The worldwide mission of the gospel has its foundation in the entire Old Testament. Upon this basis rests the whole notion of missions. The Scriptures do not distinguish between an era of salvation when God visits the Gentiles "to take out of them a people for his name" and an era following it when "the residue of men" and "all the Gentiles" "might seek after the Lord." The two are one and the same era of salvation. James quotes Amos to prove that God's visitation of the Gentiles is that foretold by the prophetic Scriptures. If this is not true, the Old Testament does not foresee the present era of salvation, and worldwide evangelization does not have any foundation in the Old Testament.

8. *Israel.*

The Messianic kingdom in which the hope of Israel centered has been established in spite of Israel's rejection of it. On account of this unbelief the nation was rejected by God. God is able to graft them in again. Their being grafted in is conditioned on repentance. Converted Jews become a part of the church; for the church holds within its scope the entirety of Old Testament teaching centering in the New Covenant and the Messianic kingdom.

If this is not true, converted Israel constitutes the Messianic kingdom and forms a separate body of saved distinct from the church. The church is thus entirely severed from the Messianic kingdom.

9. *The method of God's effecting the salvation of men.*

The Bible presents only one way of being saved. Uniformly it is taught that salvation is effected by the grace of God through the redemption that is in Christ and that it is conditioned on repentance, faith, and obedience. Further the entire human race is under probation similar to that of Adam and Eve and all must enter into the conflict against the devil. No portion of humanity at any time in world history is relieved from the battle against sin and temptation. Still further, while God sends judgment upon sinful men in order to lead them to repentance, men continue to be free moral agents able to resist the grace of God.

The alternative to this is the teaching that in a future age God will "compel" men to accept the gospel, also that He will then deal with them "*en masse* in matters pertaining to salvation." Further, it is held that during the "millennium" mankind will be relieved of all temptation by Satan.

10. *The effectiveness of the gospel.*

The Bible clearly presents the nature of the spiritual conflict in the world and of its issue. First, it teaches the adequacy and finality of the gospel as based on the finished work of Christ. The facts of redemption, of Christ's enthronement, of the outpouring of the Holy Spirit, and of the establishing of the Christian church, represent the utmost that God can do to save men. Second, the Bible presents the picture of the intensifying of the conflict between the church and the forces of evil and that the conflict will continue until the end of the world. Third, the Bible predicts the apostasy of many from the faith, but that the gates of hell shall not prevail against the church. Fourth, at the time of our Lord's return both righteous and unrighteous people will be found in the world.

Divergences from this interpretation follow at least two different paths. On the one side is the body of beliefs which holds (1) that the church is the instrument of salvation for this age only, and that it is to be superseded by the kingdom of Christ as a more effective instrument in an age to come; and (2) that the departure from the faith will increase until the church is more or less entirely apostate, or in the words of the parable of the leaven, "till the whole was leavened."

On the other side is the body of beliefs which holds (1) that the gospel will ultimately effect the salvation of mankind in general; (2) that the church will finally triumph over all her foes; and (3) that Christ will return to a saved world.

Questions

1. What were the purposes of the predictions found in the Bible?
2. What lessons could God's people learn from the fulfillment of the prophecies?
3. How do we discern what biblical language is literal and what is figurative?
4. Give some guidelines for interpreting figurative language.

5. Does the Bible contain any allegorical language? If so, give some examples.
6. Explain the expressions, kingdom of God and kingdom of heaven.
7. Do the Scriptures teach that Christ established the Messianic kingdom?
8. What is the relation between the church and Christ's kingdom?
9. What bearing does the outpouring of the Holy Spirit have on the fulfillment of prophecy?
10. Give biblical grounds for believing that Christ's return is imminent.
11. What period of time does Revelation, chapters 4 to 19 hold in view?
12. Show the harmony between the Book of Revelation and the other New Testament books.
13. What were the views of Menno Simons on the prophetic Scriptures?
14. What position does the *Mennonite Confession of Faith* hold with regard to the time of Christ's Messianic reign?
15. Set forth some of the fundamental issues involved in the interpretation of the prophetic Scriptures.

Bibliography

SELECTED BIBLIOGRAPHY

The presentation of a selected bibliography on a highly controversial subject involves a number of problems. In fairness to all views a bibliography should present works representative of every shade of interpretation. In this brief work this becomes impossible. For fuller book lists the reader is referred to the works of Hendriksen and Rutgers given below. Since this is a subject on which many different opinions exist, one must be willing to maintain an open mind on what others regard as biblical truth. I have sought to include only such authors who claim to build their eschatology wholly on the Scriptures and to be evangelical. Each work must stand, however, on its own merits.

Premillennial Works
Commentaries on the New Testament

Alford, Henry, *The Greek Testament.*

Bengel, John Albert, *Gnomon of the New Testament.*

Erdman, Charles R., *Commentary on the New Testament.*

Newell, William R., *The Book of the Revelation* (Chicago: Moody Press, 1935).

Smith, J. B., *A Revelation of Jesus Christ* (Scottdale: Herald Press, 1961).

Tenney, Merrill C., *Interpreting Revelation* (Grand Rapids: William B. Eerdmans Publishing Company, 1959).

Walvoord, John F., *The Revelation of Jesus Christ* (Chicago: Moody Press, 1966).

Monographs

Andrews, S. J., *Christianity and Anti-Christianity in Their Final Conflict,* 1898.

Blackstone, W. E., *Jesus Is Coming,* 3rd Revision, 1908. (Possibly the most frequently quoted premillennial work.) (New York: Revell, 1908).

Bonar, Horatius, *The Coming and Kingdom of the Lord Jesus Christ,* 1849.

Brookes, James H., *Maranatha or the Lord Cometh,* 10th Ed., 1889.

Chafer, Lewis S., *The Kingdom in History and Prophecy,* 6th Ed., 1926. (Strongly dispensational.)

Erdman, Charles R., *The Return of Christ,* 1922.

─────────, "Parousia" (Premillennial view), *International Standard Bible Encyclopaedia.* (A scholarly presentation.)

Feinberg, Charles, *Premillennialism or Amillennialism*. (Strongly dispensational.)

Gaebelein, A. C., *The Harmony of the Prophetic Word*, 7th Ed., 1907.

———, *Revelation*, 1915.

———, *The Return of the Lord*, 1925.

Gordon, A. J., *Ecce Venit*, 1899.

Gray, James M., *Prophecy and Lord's Return* (New York: Revell, 1917).

———, *A Text Book on Prophecy*, 3rd Ed., 1918.

Kraus, C. Norman, *Dispensationalism in America* (Richmond: John Knox Press: 1958).

Kromminga, D. H., *The Millennium: Its Nature and Function*, 1949. Covenantal Millennialism (Grand Rapids: Eerdmans, 1948).

———, *Millennium in the Church*, 1945. Covenantal Millennialism.

Moorehead, William G., "Millennium" (Premillennial view), *International Standard Bible Encyclopaedia*, 1929. (A scholarly presentation.)

Murray, George L., *Millennial Studies* (Grand Rapids: Baker Book House, 1948).

Ottman, Ford C., *The Unfolding of the Ages*, 1905.

Payne, J. Barton, *The Imminent Appearing of Christ* (Grand Rapids: William B. Eerdmans Publishing Company, 1962).

Reese, Alexander, *The Approaching Advent of Christ*, 1937. An examination of Darbyism. (Marshall, Morgan and Scott, L.T.D., London).

Ross, J. J., *Daniel's Half-Week Now Closing*, 1922.

———, *Our Glorious Hope*, 1922.

Scofield, C. I., *Reference Bible*, 1909. (Strongly dispensational.)

Seiss, J. A., *The Last Times*, 1878.

Torrey, Reuben A., *The Return of the Lord Jesus*, 1913.

Amillennial and Postmillennial Works

Since adherents of these two schools of interpretation agree on the present Messianic reign of Christ and His return for final judgment, it is not always clear to which school a given writer belongs. Amillennialists do not believe that Christ returns to a saved world nor that there shall be a thousand-year reign of peace just prior to His coming. Strict postmillennialism is giving way in two directions: on the one side, to a loose interpretation of the thousand years which looks to a general triumph of Christ's reign in bringing all men to repentance; and on the other, to amillennialism as expressing more accurately the creedal position of historic Christianity as set forth in the Apostles' Creed, namely, His present Messianic reign and His return for judgment.

Commentaries on the New Testament

Clarke, Adam, *The Holy Bible . . . with a Commentary and Critical Notes.*

Cook, F. C., Editor, *The Holy Bible with Commentary.*

Henry, Matthew, *An Exposition of the Old and New Testaments.*

Lenski, R. C. H., *Commentary on the New Testament.*

Whedon, D. D., *Commentary on the Bible.*

Commentaries on the Revelation

Blaney, Harvey J. S., The Wesleyan Bible Commentary, Vol. Six, "Revelation" (Grand Rapids: William B. Eerdmans Publishing Company, 1966), pp. 402-523.

Caird, G. B., *A Commentary on the Revelation of St. John, the Divine* (New York: Harper & Row Publishers, 1966).

Richardson, Donald W., *The Revelation of Jesus Christ* (Richmond: John Knox Press, 1939).

Scott, C. Anderson, *The Book of the Revelation* (London: Hodder and Stoughton, 1905).

Swete, Henry Barclay, *The Apocalypse of St. John* (Grand Rapids: William B. Eerdmans Publishing Company, 1908).

Monographs

Allis, Oswald T., *Prophecy and the Church*, 1945 (Presbyterian and Reformed Publishing Company, Philadelphia, Pa.).

Bales, James D., *The New Testament Interpretation of Old Testament Prophecies of the Kingdom* (Searcy: The Harding College Press, 1950).

Boettner, Loraine, *The Millennium* (Grand Rapids, Baker Book House, 1958). Presents all three views of the Millennium.

Brown, David, *The Second Advent*, 1849. (Postmillennial.)

Hamilton, Floyd E., *The Basis of Millennial Faith* (Grand Rapids: William B. Eerdmans Publishing Company, 1942). (Amillennial; a splendid work written in nontechnical language by a conservative scholar.)

Hendriksen, W., *More Than Conquerors*, 3rd Ed., 1944. (Amillennial.)

Landis, Ira D., *The Faith of Our Fathers on Eschatology* (Lititz, Pa., published by the author, 1946).

Masselink, William, *Why Thousand Years*, 1930. (Amillennial.)

Mauro, Philip, *The Gospel of the Kingdom* (Boston: Hamilton Brothers, 1928).

———, *The Hope of Israel*, 1929. (Amillennial.)

Milligan, W., *The Book of Revelation*, 1889.

———, *Discussions on the Apocalypse*, 1893. (Postmillennial.)

Mueller, John Theodore, "Parousia" (Postmillennial view), *International Standard Bible Encyclopaedia*, 1929. (A very scholarly presentation, in reality Amillennial in viewpoint.)

Rall, H. F., *Modern Premillennialism and the Christian Hope*, 1920.

Richardson, Donald W., *The Revelation of Jesus Christ*, 1939. (Amillennial.)

Rutgers, W. H., *Premillennialism in America*, 1930.

Stafford, T. P., *A Study of the Kingdom*, 1925. (Amillennial.)

Vos, Geerhardus, *The Pauline Eschatology*, 1930.

———: "Eschatology in the New Testament," *International Standard Bible Encyclopaedia*, 1929. (The most scholarly presentation of the Amillennial viewpoint.)

Wyngaarden, Martin J., *The Future of the Kingdom in Prophecy and Fulfillment* (Grand Rapids: Zondervan Publishing House, 1934).

The Author

Chester K. Lehman was born near Millersville, Pennsylvania. A graduate of First Pennsylvania State Normal School, he continued his education receiving an AB from Hesston College and Bible School, AM from Franklin and Marshall College, ThB from Princeton Theological Seminary, and ThM, ThD from Union Theological Seminary, Richmond, Virginia.

He served as dean of Eastern Mennonite College from 1924-1956, as head of the Bible Department from 1921-1965, and has continued part-time service as professor of theology in the seminary. His teaching field included New Testament Greek exegesis, English Bible, Christian ethics, and theology (biblical and systematic).

He is the author of *The Inadequacy of Evolution as a World View*, *Bible Survey Course (N. T. Studies)*, *The Holy Spirit and the Holy Life*, and *Biblical Theology of the Old Testament*. Unpublished theses include: *The Conception of Personality and Its Theological Applications*, *Prolegomena to Christian Theology*, and *The Teaching of the Bible on the Last Things*.

He shared in the writing of *The Revised Standard Version, An Examination and Evaluation; Mennonite Confession of Faith;* and in compiling *The Mennonite Hymnal*.

He is an ordained minister and has held several pastorates in his local area. He has served in Bible conferences throughout the Mennonite Church.